OLIVIA'S SHOPPING

AND

How She Does It

A PREJUDICED GUIDE TO THE LONDON SHOPS

GUNPOWDER PRESS 2009

Published by Gunpowder Press,
Stroud, Gloucestershire, UK

First published in 1906

ISBN 978-0-9562450-0-7

Printed in India by Imago Ltd

Olivia and her Shopping

Charles Mosley

Who was Olivia, author of *Olivia's Shopping*? She gives no surname. She almost certainly wasn't the 'Olivia' who, confusingly, wrote a novel called *Olivia* and in real life was Dorothy Bussy, Lytton Strachey's sister. Mind you, the dates fit. 'Olivia'/Dorothy Bussy was around forty when *Olivia's Shopping* was published, so would have known the West End retail outlets as our Olivia does. But our Olivia has a more esoteric prose style, almost like Gertrude Stein's.

She may have been American-born, as Stein was. She writes much of her book for Americans, refers often to American retailing practices, and once uses the American 'outside of' rather than 'outside'. American origins would fit. A pioneer consumerist, operating fifty years before *Which?* was established, she is almost the Ralph Nader of Edwardian London's emporia.

And 'emporia', though highfalutin, is the word. Department stores were to fashionable pre-1914 era women, then just embarking on emancipation, what clubs had long been to men. Inside a department store a woman was protected from street life, with its rough crowds, beggars, and muck thrown up by bustling hansom cabs. She was protected, too, from home life, with its tiresome servants, numerous children, and the boredom of having all domestic work taken off her hands. To us that might seem no hardship, but many of the neuroses Freud had so recently catalogued often arose from just such female bourgeois ennui.

Emporia offered not just shopping but also tea-rooms, restaurants, the servile attention of frock-coated floor-walkers, perhaps a flirtation, certainly the chance to meet friends. Literature of the period abounds in shopping episodes, from Saki's short stories to E. M. Forster's *Howards End.*

In Osbert Lancaster's *All Done From Memory*, describing his Bayswater childhood, Whiteley's, the district's main shop, is virtually a temple to his female relatives. It supplies them with every household need, draws them on frequent visits (as much of inspection as of purchase), and provides them with the material for endless gossip in an age before celebrity magazines and soap operas.

Sadly, Whiteley's is no more. Nor are Derry & Toms, Dickins & Jones, Marshall & Snelgrove, or Swan & Edgar. Debenhams, Harvey Nichols, Liberty and Harrods thrive. But Barkers is gone too. So is Bourne

& Hollingsworth the shop, though a retro-themed niche bar with the same name occupies its site and strives to recreate a 'period' atmosphere. Olivia would have liked that.

Further reading

Alison Adburgham, *Shops and Shopping, 1880–1914* (1964, 2nd edn 1981)

Alison Adburgham, *Victorian Shopping* (1972)

Alexandra Artley (ed.), *The Golden Age of Shop Design: European Shop Interiors 1880–1939* (1975)

Sean Callery, *Harrods Knightsbridge: The Story of Society's Favourite Store* (1991)

Maurice Corina, *Fine Silks and Oak Counters, Debenhams 1778–1978* (1978)

Tim Dale, *Harrods: The Store and the Legend* (1981)

A. Stuart Gray, *Edwardian Architecture: A Biographical Dictionary* (1985)

Richard S. Lambert, *The Universal Provider, A Study of William Whiteley and the Rise of the London Department Store* (1938)

Alison Settle, *A Family of Shops* (1951)

FOREWORD

To Advertisers

THIS book is written from the outside. Whatever is in it is genuine.

Your business is not touched on in detail; it is merely talked, gossiped about in an informal manner. Criticism is offered in generalities, commendation in particulars.

If you want full particulars of your business to become known to the reader you must advertise. A place in the index will be afforded you on this understanding, and the position of your house indicated on a map to be included in the volume.

CONTENTS

FOREWORD

To the Frequent Visitor

EVERY woman in London has her shopping code, or else she is acquiring one. Everybody is willing to have tips, and there is no official mode of obtaining these.

Shops should be criticised like pictures or plays; instead, they are merely boomed in advertisement.

The libel laws prevent abuse of particular shops, of course, but there is no reason why one may not, in drawing attention to the special benefits to be obtained in others, effect a very useful critical handbook on London shops.

This book is, above all things, to appear genuine, so that it may be something worth while for a firm to be mentioned in it. I am strongly of opinion that very few women are at all impressed with the vapid flatteries of shops to be seen in ladies' papers, and simply ripe for a shop Baedeker which discriminates and choses for them.

There is not a hint in the book which has not been discovered through experience—from the buyer's point of view.

There are numberless little things to be said publicly regarding the London shops which no one seems to have the courage to put into ladies' papers. These will be taken full notice of in the reflections of Olivia.

If you have a disinterested good friend in London, who knows well how to dress, let me warn you—you do not require this book. For, over the teacups, you have, in all certainty, discussed the very things which make it, and have, no doubt, already formed your own opinions on the subject.

Likewise, if you are of unlimited means, there is no wisdom in your tracking the course of less fortunate people throughout this volume. For you have only to enter the gilded and white doors of any splendid establishment in the vicinity of Bond Street, and your belief in the simplicity of London shopping is complete.

But for those of you who are not so very wealthy, and before the disinterested friend appeared, what would you not have given, in the first instance, to have known all you know now of the London shops?

Do you remember the period when you went delightedly to order a ten-guinea gown in ——, and had as encouragement to your enthusiasm: 'Madam, we could make a *sleeve* for that amount'?

Or do you ever happen to recollect the dark, sad days when you had not heard of the Dickens' and Jones Tea-room?

London, that happy hunting-ground for the very wealthy, is, on occasion, a wilderness to the less wealthy. Yet, to the woman who knows her London, there is not a more moderate and satisfactory shopping place in the world. And daily it becomes more comfortable.

There is no reason why everyone at the start should not obtain the friendly tips which are available from the person on the spot, especially when these may be had so easily, and in the shortest moment of time—even in the train running to London—from such a book as this.

I do not pretend to an exhaustive résumé of all the good things to be had in the London shops. For in that case my helpful book might become as distracting as the ladies' papers, and as bewildering as the shops themselves.

I merely thread a path formed by individual experience in the matter of buying clothes in London, and of the most convenient ways of setting about it. My remarks on dress, therefore, will be much mingled with advice as to bus fares, temptations to tea-rooms, and sidelights on luncheon places. For these, I find, are necessary to the completion of the successful shopping day.

Herewith are therefore dedicated to you, for your use and wise preferment, the economical reflections of

OLIVIA.

Chapter I

Regent Street

REGENT STREET is the beautiful white gateway to London. You have to get to it sometime, since every ambitious omnibus route lands you there sooner or later. And you have to pass through it, if only to acquire your focus with regard to shopping in London.

There, in the region of the smartest, you may find at the same time the most moderate and efficient things for ordinary life. And for a vicinity which combines these advantages, there are smaller chances of buying trash in Regent Street than in any street in London.

Peter Robinson's, at the top, is hall-marked with the same air of confidence that one bestows on the Tower of London and similar institutions. Certain things are to be found there, we know, and nothing, as a rule, occurs to disturb our belief. This firm, time-honoured and diligent, came triumphantly out of what I should call the black silk period in dress, the period in which Peter Robinson's became famous, and now offer what to most women must seem a dazzling assortment of modern smart things. But what I find most delightful in Peter Robinson's is the latent stability of the Victorian Era still backing our more flimsy modern one. In the matter of choosing woollen things, for instance, one may only, at the best of times, remain a good amateur. At Peter Robinson's are the experts. These are trained people, who discriminate scientifically between cotton and wool, and tell you the truth about it—not languid persons of many manners and no knowledge, who will swear cotton is silk to have done with you.

If Peter Robinson's say that things will wear well, they generally do. If you get a costume there which you like well in the first instance, a happy satisfaction in it abides with you to its close. I have always liked in particular the cut of the ready-made skirts and coats to be had at Peter Robinson's; they seem to me to have something more than the usual haphazard grace of the manufacturer's achievement about them. Also I make a point of Peter Robinson's for sailor and travelling hats of all descriptions; these seem always so especially tasteful and right. With regard to the two houses of Peter Robinson's—Regent and Oxford Street—your one friend will advise you to Regent Street, and the next—quite as well informed—will at once mention Oxford Street. After all it is only

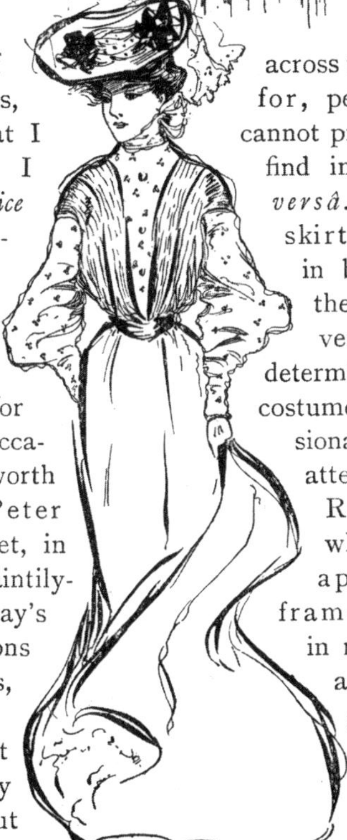

the difference of across the street in most instances, for, personally, I find that what I cannot procure in Regent Street I find in Oxford Street, and *vice versâ*. For fluffy silk under-skirts and great variety in blouses I have found the Oxford Street house very useful. But I can never determine which I like best for costumes. Both houses have occasional sales, which are well worth attending.

Opposite Peter Robinson's in Regent Street, in white magnificence, the daintily-appointed windows of Jay's frame their latest confections in millinery, gloves, parasols, and shoes, in a manner generally unique in Regent Street. I am giving my economical reflections, but I must drop a passing sigh regretting the circumstances which, except for certain trifles, keep me out of Jay's. There is only one standard in Jay's, and that is what is easiest understood as exclusiveness. I do not call their confections expensive, I merely say they are of one grade of excellence. Skilled artistic work goes into every gown; embroidery by hand is applied in the most perfect fashion. These can never be too well paid for in my opinion, and the fashionable woman invariably gets something in Jay's which is an actual work of art. For those of us who are unable to reckon our gowns by the twenty guineas, however, there are still things to be had at Jay's. Daintily clocked, embroidered and open-work stockings, well-fitting gloves, parasols—these, when I want them exceptionally pretty and of uncommon design, I endeavour to buy at Jay's.

I have invariably the belief that a successful business does not become successful by any streak of luck or through any mere arrangement of Providence. Success is the result of talent and genius, and Dickens and Jones, next in order in Regent Street, I am well convinced must be the result of its lace counter. I am lured to that edifice, times without number, by means of a seductive window of lace, which always seems to offer me some one thing a little more desirable and unusual than the rest of shops of this calibre. I refer both to real and imitation lace, also to chiffons, trimmings, ruchings, rufflings, waist-belts, flower garnitures, clasps and buttons, all of which have really the appearance of being selected by a person of artistic judgment. Here I have had made up for me at various times different fichus and ruffles in lace and chiffon which I found impossible to acquire ready-made. The cut of the Dickens and Jones blouses, moreover, is a sure thing, and makes their handiwork in this connection worth the little increase in price evident over the usual shop blouse.

Liberty's, world renowned and near at hand, must be credited with having helped London out of the hard, starchy, black silk period, establishing a fashion in dress stuffs and dress design, of which the soft lines, the crêpe-de-chine effects of the present day are merely a delicious development. Nowadays, the best results of modern British art are offered to Liberty, who less and less seem to be compelled to confine themselves to eastern manufacture. There is also more artistic competition among the other shops than there ever was formerly. Never the less, for a particular shade of brown cloth I found Liberty's still pre-eminent. They had every imaginable tone in soft, satisfying shades. For tea-gowns and dinner-gowns I commend Liberty's. For children's gowns and hats it is perfection. Special and beautiful consignments from abroad of such things as crêpe and silk embroidered shawls, kimonos, etc., make Liberty's exceptional among shops of this description.

Robinson and Cleaver, besides the usual attractions of an Irish house, offer particular temptations in original blouses, crash and linen skirts, well made and quite unstereotyped in design. There one may choose materials for a certain pattern in blouses and have it made to order in Ireland. Lace and gloves are to be had in most excellent quality, washing-gloves being especially good.

At Piccadilly Circus occurs Swan and Edgars. For the actual size of the shop itself, I consider the Swan and Edgars windows the most comprehensive in Regent Street. Everything of consequence is in them, including the prices, and many times the waiting for an omnibus has shown me a much-sought article lying there ready to be bought. This house seems to make a speciality of unmade robes, or skirts ready-made with material to match, both at very moderate prices. There is also a perfectly-fascinating haberdashery counter, while for real lace at most reasonable figures, I consider that Swan and Edgar offer quite the best opportunity in London.

As an offshoot from Piccadilly, two shops in the vicinity ought to be visited. One, Stagg and Mantle's, at Leicester Square, I find particularly enticing in lace scarfs, silk skirts, etc. And Russell's, in Wardour Street, immediately behind, is one of the unique places in London. For this reason, that nearly every London woman who shops in this district of Regent Street refers you sooner or later to the particular cut of gloves, or the fine selection of hats, or the assortment of beautiful *lingerie* to be had at Russell's. It is a shop, which, once patronized for any of these things, is seldom dropped into forgetfulness.

A résumé of Regent Street would put this busy shopping district as a spot where a fair price is asked for a good article. At certain portions, it is true, Bond Street may be said to have leaked in. The charm of Lewis and Allenby, of Ernest, of Jay's may be counted as of hybrid excellence in the white spaciousness of Regent Street. But even in these, where material is to be had by the yard, it is often quite moderate in price and nearly always lovely.

On the whole, you may clothe yourself very economically in Regent Street; but you may not clothe yourself cheaply. In this white quarter a superb distinction is drawn between the meanings of these two words.

Chapter II

Oxford Street

IF Regent Street is for the woman who can pay, Oxford Street is for the woman who can afford to make mistakes.

There are plenty of chances for extravagance in Oxford Street—these not alone in expensive places. Oxford Street ought to be avoided by anyone who is easily attracted by the sleek, vainglorious outward appearance of earthly vanities.

Because you have paid fifty guineas for a charming cloak in one shop, there is no reason why next door you may not find a badly fittting blouse for 1s. 6¾d. Extremes unknown in Regent Street meet in Oxford Street. You may buy anything, from an elevenpenny hat to the last thing in Parisian toilets.

If regrets are to be made afterwards it is generally on account of the elevenpenny hat. This is rather a crude manner of attack on the part of fate, but I find it a common result of Oxford Street.

Yet if you forego the temptations of buying a thing merely because it is cheap, Oxford Street has far more opportunities in a certain direction than Regent Street. It is primarily for the woman who adapts, offering endless variety of choice in almost every department of millinery and dressmaking. And pre-eminent among the very fine shops of London stand some of those in Oxford Street.

For a good range of superior silks and dress stuffs at deserving prices, commend me to Marshall and Snell-grove's, and I do not know that any house can offer quite such de-licious delaines, summer gauzes, etc., as I have over and over again discovered here. There is a quiet, even taste pervading everything in Marshall and Snell-groves, which stamps every article with the hall-mark of special value.

Evan's, quite near, is a busy place, and

one of the most alluring shops I know. Hats and trimmings for hats, trimmings of all sorts, under-skirts of endless variety—for these I should always much recommend Evans's. But beyond everything, I like this house for dressing sacques, gowns, etc., a department devoted to these being well worth a special visit. Everywhere throughout Evans's you will be tempted with side issues, for both within the two shops and the subway connecting them, departments alien to the subject of dress invitingly disport themselves.

Lewis's, still in the same vicinity, is a first-rate place for trimmings of all descriptions.

Harries's, I like for untrimmed hats especially, and a perfectly marvellous selection of flowers to choose from for trimming these.

Penberthy's is practically indispensable to the well-equipped woman for a very carefully chosen and special stock of underwear, haberdashery of all sorts, gloves, veils, etc. This, more than any firm of the same importance in London, makes almost a separate business of such things.

The nearer to Edgeware Road, the nearer become the shops to the standards required by the busy and teeming populace living round that most energetic highway to the north-west of London. Our path slides back again towards Tottenham Court Road, and on the way picks up that treasure-house of distracting opportunity in the way of laces, hats, veils, etc., Bourne and Hollingsworth. There are residents in the vicinity of Westbourne Grove whose life has become a blank to them since Bourne and Hollingsworth moved from their midst into the extreme end of Oxford Street. Certainly for variety in ordinary lace, fichus, flowers, etc., this place is deservedly a great favourite.

For whoever wants something unusual in silk, lace, etc., Lewis's silk-market in Holborn ought never to be forgotten. This house seems to have a faculty for procuring things which do not appear to reach the ordinary shops for the delectation of the middle-classes. In the prevailing scramble for the article of the moment, every shop seeks to produce only the very latest. The results is that most shops in their various vicinities become very much alike. This is not to be said of Lewis's, where I invariably go to be helped out of a matching dilemma, to find silk for a gown of a pattern not joyfully smiling from every street corner in London—and for linings! Lewis's is invaluable for silk linings.

Shoolbred's, in Tottenham Court Road, ought to be mentioned here. It is quite one of the best shops in London. It runs steadily on as an effectual supply to the needs of good family people, and the quality of its stock never varies from the best. I should advise anyone who is buying costume cloth to buy it at Shoolbred's. I never saw such variety in dark blues, for instance, as I have seen there. Also there is a particularly enticing counter for buckles, waist-belts, etc.

As a quiet offshoot to Oxford Street, Wigmore Street seems to have chosen and assorted the finer things out of that busy, haphazard assortment running parallel behind it. Here are shops of small appearance but of very first-rate quality, with Debenham and Freebody as a giant among them setting a standard of the best. For good and splendid furs, I should, first of all houses, try Debenham's. They cater, too, for the wants of most people in less important things, and a special kind of black suede glove, which they sell at 1s. 11½d., has made this shop a favourite with many quite economically-minded people.

Chapter III

Bond Street

No woman should enter Bond Street for shopping purposes who is not prepared some time or another to pay half-a-crown for tea.

This price guages the street. One must remember that there is not much room in Bond Street even for pedestrians. Customers are therefore chosen carefully. All who cannot pay for gilded, padded daintiness must consent to remain middle-class spectators of the achievements of Bond Street. If it contents you, on the other hand, to take tea in an immature lighthouse, each tiny floor a mere bijou, rose-coloured, lattice-windowed cosy-corner; sugar-tongs in pink ribbon—I always wonder why the lumps are not also confiscated to decoration of this sort—faded music in the basement, then you may be very happy in Bond Street. For myself I prefer fresh air, and more of it. But the only open spaces in Bond Street seem to be reserved for fish and poultry.

In ordering a gown or buying a hat, one must remember these things—that the very space one takes up for the moment is reckoned in pounds and shillings; that the air one breathes is made of gold. One has to pay for loving a place in these hard, mercenary times, and one has invariably to pay for being happy in Bond Street. Regent Street is for wealthy suburbians and Bayswater, Oxford Street is for the world, but Bond Street is for princes and Park Lane.

The admirable manner in which the highest in the land consent to be crowded into a picture show, for instance; the care one has to devote to original and wonderfully-varied curb-stones; the neat way one avoids knocking into a duke; and, above all, the price one has to pay for a toque—these must convince the ordinary mortal that Bond Street is for the elect.

Nevertheless, from the spectacular point of view, there is an enchantment in the very discomforts of Bond Street which is unparalleled in Europe or America, and if everyone could quite afford the beautiful things reservedly showing themselves in the windows, this book should never have been written.

On the other hand, just as the ethics of Bond Street have filtered into Regent Street, so the standard of Regent Street has in certain places invaded Bond Street.

In Walpole's Irish Linen House, for instance, all sorts of beautiful teacloths, hand-embroidered blouses, stocks, collars, etc., are just as reasonable and excellent in Bond Street as in any shop out of it.

Certain milliners, too, make a point of producing hats and toques at most moderate figures. Madame Tucker Widgery is well-known in this way.

Corke's is a very favourite house with many people for blouses, while Redmayne's, as a general establishment, seems to me to give a more generous choice to customers than one might expect from the traditions of Bond Street. Also there are the Glove and Shoe Companies, who may be said to cater for everyone.

Still, I maintain that Bond Street, in its ordinary aspects, must be treated by the middle-class woman with reserve. It is one of the most charming, sparkling byways in the whole world. But whoever does business in its quaint, crowded environment, must either rise or succumb to its responsibilities and inevitable consequences.

Chapter IV

Sloane Street and Knightsbridge

I MAY be wrong, but to me the sun always seems to be shining in Sloane Street.

To be a perfectly happy woman, one ought to go shopping there in the morning. It is Bond Street with the air let in. The very blouses seem to gather inspiration from the deliciousness around them—the pretty irregular houses, the green gardens, the flower-studded balconies. To be gowned in Sloan Street—this means satisfaction with the world in general. Nothing can really go wrong with the woman who wears a Sloane Street blouse. From Knightsbridge to that flower-studded residential part, shops of unpretential dimensions offer the most charming things, especially blouses. There is an air attached to each article—it is stamped with dainty handiwork which can only be described as expressing Sloane Street.

I should advise every woman who can afford it to shop in Sloane Street, for there is no such pleasant and satisfying place in the world.

And although this is by no means a cheap shopping district, I hold that it is not unduly influenced by exclusiveness in the matter of price. There, I am not so much aware that I am paying for high rents as for a very dainty article. In Sloane Street one pays for taste and judgment, and these, to my mind, are often worth a little sacrifice in other directions. The lowest street average I should put at 10s. 6d. for a shirt blouse, two guineas for a dressy one, fifteen guineas for a costume. With that standard in your mind, you may enjoy Sloane Street, and even find that, on occasion, this locality meets a more economical standpoint. In Lee's, for instance, one of the nicest shops in Sloane Street, hats and toques are sold at three prices—21s., 25s., and 30s.—none of these exorbitant at any time, far less so in a pretty hat redolent of Sloane Street.

Head's, in this vicinity, is an invaluable shop for materials and patterns of all sorts of knitting, crochetting, and embroidery. Here one may acquire particulars and equipment for making waistcoats, jerseys, etc., stringing beads, and so on.

Catts' specializes in haberdashery of all descriptions, and is a splendid place for different kinds of elaborate and picturesque trimmings, veils, buttons, etc.

And although photo-frames ought not to come into a booklet which discourses on clothes, it is impossible to pass Jones' in Sloane Street without wanting to buy some of these things.

For blouses, veils, and gloves of the daintiest make, I recommend Sands as the right place, *par excellence.* There is something distinctive about everything to be bought here.

Goodmans', for a certain type of tailor-made looking blouse, and for a specially-priced hat at 30s., is excellent.

Dresses and blouses at Samson's have just the right delicious Sloane Street cut, colour, and air which one at once distinguishes, and in which one at once delights.

Addley Bourne is another Sloane Street name with which to conjure dreams of colour and dainty elegance. For children's things this place is charming.

And once more back to veils, and to Sangers' across the way, for most of these shops have followed in quick succession on one side of Sloane Street. There one finds a shop expert in the minor accompaniments to a perfect toilet.

All these for the woman who reaches Sloane Street; but I warn the visitor that, if she makes her way in the first instance by Knightsbridge, she may never want to go further. There are people living in the vicinity of Sloane Street who would think that the world were well lost were Harvey Nicol's not in it. With something like real affection they do their shopping in 'Harvey's,' and would as soon think of trading in Camberwell as removing their allegiance elsewhere. This shop is exceptionally first-rate, and as a side issue I must mention the pretty pieces of brocade to be had here for cushions, etc.

Woolland's, next door—I may as well confess it—is my favourite shop in London. Although I have only a buying acquaintance with the place, I am certain of one thing in connection with it: someone is at the head of affairs who has a most delicious sense of colour. The very carpets on the floors at Woollands give this away. When this deliciousness runs into ribbons and chiffon, one may imagine the result. I should certainly go to Woolland's for most things in the matter of dress, if one could always afford beautiful things. As it is, I take every opportunity of buying flowers, veils, chiffon, stocks, silk, and dress stuff in that pretty place. It is unique in ideas, and yet, for unmade things, quite within the reach of moderate purchasers. Dressmaking is on a prohibitive scale for some people, who yet may find ready-made costumes, and at least always the material for the making of others, in the sweetest profusion, at Woolland's.

Chapter V

Highways Beyond

High Street, Kensington; Westbourne Grove; Buckingham Palace Road

It is a curious fact that the West of London, so far as shopping is concerned, centres in Regent Street. Out of this real 'West'—yet very much of it—are tributaries of fashion, shopping-places of note and real interest.

High Street, Kensington, for instance, more west in point of geography than Regent Street, yet not always included in the popular shopping acceptance of the word, is one of the happiest hunting-grounds for the shopping enthusiast. It is the nicest, prettiest, cosiest corner in London. There is a sense of fine out-of-door pleasure in the very look of the place. Picturesque, leisured, artistic people thread their way in and out of the crowds there, and there are more perambulators and more pretty babies on the pavement than on any area of the same restrictions in the Metropolis. Kensington Gardens are to be held responsible for the babies; and the turn of Camden Hill, the winding way of the High Street, and the beautiful sense of proportion which made old Kensington lovely and New Kensington possible, have added just that effect of comfort and compactness which foretells that every shop in such a vicinity will easily be successful. There is really nothing quite so important as environment, and the environment of Kensington is very nearly perfect so far as the shops in High Street are concerned.

Therefore it is worth a morning— or more — even if one does not live in Kensington. There is Barker's, for instance, with a perfectly unique silk counter. Everything there is good, and encouragingly reasonable, with seasonable baits of French silks, which are irresistible. A splendid place for silk voiles, crepons, Japanese silks, patterned things of unusual workmanship. There is a clever person somewhere in the establishment who must be congratulated on a providential eye kept on the silk market. This statement is based on many satisfying memories of the silk department in Barker's. Blouses are interesting here, and the lace department is also worth travelling to.

There are quite a number of people who look up the lace department periodically, just as one would step into a first-rate picture-gallery every now and again, for the pure delight of finding the newest nice thing, and the purring contentment of believing that it might easily not be had so reasonably elsewhere. A length of silk, a lace berthe (and a Madeira cake), at Barker's! I see these familiar outstanding excellencies always in my mind's eye.

Derry and Toms, having lately added a most charming and delightfully-lit salon to their establishment, make shopping inside their white walls a comfort and a pleasure. One feels drawn at once to speak of hats, for they are everywhere, it would seem, at one particular wide gallery—hats in graded prices, from 10s. 9d. to anything you please. These hats have been made too specially competitive with the other things in this warehouse to be passed over lightly. I bought the best fur collar and muff I ever possessed in Derry and Toms'.

Their dressmaking is delightful; underclothing especially good; hatpins, hair-combs, etc., fascinating

Ponting's, still in procession with the others, another well-equipped storehouse of 'everything,' makes a speciality of church embroidery, and often may be relied upon to supply an unusual demand. Under clothing, especially, is most varied and reasonable.

High Street is rich in luncheon and tea rooms, detailed in another chapter.

It is possible to take a bus from Kensington—the much-loved 'blue one'—over to one of the unique places of London. Westbourne Grove, that spot fondly cherished by the country of 'country orders' as some green grove in the nice-sounding coolness of a place termed Bayswater—Westbourne Grove is the poetic shopping-place of London, until one has been there, when it becomes as concrete as the town can make it, with business of the most go-ahead description in place of groves and leafiness. How one of these wonderful men in Whiteley's on a Saturday morning, shouting orders, as it seems, to a buzzing air of crowded figures, send in their orders completed, paid for, weighed and measured, is one of London's mysteries.

But this is outside of the dress question. It was a great intelligence that made Whiteley's, and it is a great intelligence that keeps it; this in spite of the fact that splendid new-century, finely-finished buildings have reared their heads, and, in the light of their enterprise, made us wonder why we were so stunned with the first of them in Whiteley's.

Whiteley's hold the market with a firm hand. They are worth watching. When you see the advertisements speak of a certain 'line' to be displayed at Westbourne Grove, run for it. Things are to be procured there at any odd time which may not be seen elsewhere in London. One does not particularize. It is 'universal providing,' and this book has its limits, so I leave Whiteley's and go on to the other opportunities.

Westbourne Grove is full of them. Across the way, for instance, is Owen's, where everything in smaller bulk seems specially selected for one, as though looked out that morning and displayed to show just the things one wants most to look at. Try this place for embroidered trimmings, pretty buttons, stoles, hats; try it for ready-made linen and summer costumes, also for Indian and foreign outfits. It is an ideal 'summer' house, in my opinion; everything always fresh, unsoiled by the London which can tarnish so easily. Ask here for embroidery silks and patterns; they are specially nice.

Courtney's, on the other side, for dresses, blouses, and hats, still work on the same basis, and many dainty things are to be had here. One is constantly being 'had over' in Westbourne Grove, first on the one side, then on the other.

Therefore, after the first plunge at Whiteley's, and the consequent rush to the other side for Owen's, etc., let us back to a dissecting tour of the Whiteley side. Dobbs', next door, from sponges to hair-nets, is a wondrous marvel of haberdashery. I dwell on hair-nets, for this is the place for them. Yet these are only incidental. If you are on an elastic-buying, odds-and-ends, hairpin-hunting expedition, go to Dobbs' in Westbourne Grove, and you'll be happy.

Also, if you are in the Swiss-embroidery, under-trimming, calico-buying mood, take each shop as it comes in Westbourne Grove and try your luck. Harries', for cycling-knickers and underskirts, please mark very distinctly. This is the thoroughfare for a complete outfit, if ever there was one.

A corset-making establishment is to be highly recommended. Wallace Taylor's, an establishment for ready-made blouses, costumes, skirts, is one of the best in London. It is only to be compared with a hat-shop next door under a similar name, where hats and toques are excellent. Ponting's, further on, I look upon as a lacy establishment of the busy, haberdashery order. Bargains in ribbons and flowers will tempt you from a brilliant window indoors, till the memory of temptations still to come tempts you out again.

One's journey ends at Bradley's, at Richmond Road, but very nicely might begin as well as end there, especially if one uses the 'blue bus.' It is a rigorously high-class establishment, where one may depend on good things at reasonable prices. For good furs at their proper value this place is pre-eminent. Costumes, also, are delightful, and dress-making to be relied upon. The splendours of 'the Grove' cease abruptly at this point. It is as well. There may be no limit to the resources of Westbourne Grove, but there is a limit to one's purse. One leaves it—for another day!

A highway, or more nearly a by-way, to be reached easily from town, and possessing just the right quiet air for successful shopping, is Buckingham Palace Road, close to Victoria Station.

Here, pre-eminent, is Gorringe's, one of the really fine shops of London. It is an establishment of the general order, and one is as pointedly tempted with photograph frames as with delicious dress stuffs. It is a firm renowned for good dressmaking, and as a Christmas place is unique for its opportunities. Go to Buckingham Palace Road for hats especially. There is Blackaller's, an invaluable place for flowers, trimmings, etc. Good tailors and shoemakers abound. It is a comprehensive by-way, neither unreasonably expensive nor suspiciously cheap. And besides the usual tea places, there are two delightfully dainty ones.

Chapter VI

The Stores

There is a portion of the London public which, in a certain instance, is entirely to be depended upon. Ask 'Where should I buy—anything?' and you know the answer before it is spoken: 'The Stores.' That splendid institution has saved many people all the ardour and dismay of a hunt through London. Everything is so nicely obtained within the walls of the Army and Navy, the machinery of the whole business is so well established, the development so complete, that it is small wonder the way of a member is an easy one, and the path of a shareholder lined with peace.

Nowadays, the rival establishments of a similar nature detract from the Stores sensation to a certain extent, but only to a certain extent. One may still rely on the Army and Navy for an evenness in pricing and a first-rate standard of quality, down to the last box of pins.

The Army and Navy, in Victoria Street, from its

picturesque doorway of dogs, being carefully looked after by a historical porter, onwards, is an institution of justice and contentment, and the care that is taken in the matter of country orders ought to be mentioned in Parliamentary returns.

I fancy they still serve tea here on archaic principles, if I remember rightly, and while it matches the virtues of constancy displayed elsewhere in this establishment, it is one point which might be conceded to the fancifulness of the times. Also, while I touch on what might now be called criticism, there is a lift in the Junior Army and Navy which does not march with the rush of progress quite so fast as many admirable details in the management of York House. This lift, I fancy, is a sort of public property, so that one may warn a stranger, I hope, and only be thanked for the information. My advice, however, in spite of lift and tea-room, to all visitors to London, if they have failed in finding the article which they want in other places, is: 'Beg, or borrow, or steal a number, and try the Stores.'

It is a country woman's impression sometimes that only hams and groceries are to be had in such establishments. They cannot imagine that tea may be bought next door to tea-gowns. It is a fact that, while there are few places, except Shoolbred's, in London, so good for bacon as the Stores, there are none more dainty for, say, summer muslins.

Try Victoria Street for organdies, and cotton voiles,

and mercerized lawns; there is no place more delightful. Try them for notepaper, and especially envelopes —envelopes of strange sizes, account-books, diaries; everything very useful in stationery is stocked to excellence at the Stores. Get your size of gloves established, and you need never go further. Get your make of shoes registered, and you may go to China and still be served with shoes from the Stores. Indeed, go anywhere throughout the world, and the benefits of the Stores will follow you. In no corner of the earth need you be without their periodical supplies. The British Parliament is one institution, the Stores are another. Only after these have been mentioned need we think of successors.

Chapter VII

To the Homesick American

I HAVE used the above title in order properly to exploit Harrod's Stores. It is impossible to imagine any stranger within our gates so happy as the American woman when she first finds herself under that stupendous roof, unless, perhaps, it is the American woman who railed against everything English before Harrod's was invented.

The Army and Navy Stores, for instance, marked an epoch in London shopping, but they never really satisfied the fair American. Some kind of enchantment drew her to the doors, however—probably the mystery of having to own, beg, or borrow a number. Americans are loyal and generous to one another; I have known one number at the Army and Navy Stores do duty to hundreds of them. Who first gave it away, or to whom it really belonged, no one knew, but they all quoted it assiduously for spun silk underwear, and dreamed of bargains. The one expression they used when walking through the place was invariably, 'Compared to the Other Side——' The rest was anti-British!

Now, the Army and Navy Stores capably introduced to London what is very nearly perfected at Harrod's, minus the membership. I, who have seen the 'Other Side,' can assure Americans that in this sumptuous building of plate-glass and red velvet they will be as much at home—if they ever desire such a consummation to their feelings—in Harrod's as anywhere in London. During the recent alterations, I began to fear that Harrod's, of which I had always been very fond, was likely to become a palace of red velvet and no merchandise. But I am wrong. It is, like its telegraphic address, 'Everything,' and becomes more enticing every minute.

The American woman especially ought to rejoice. In a place where green corn and ice-cream sodas are to be had she should surely find all that she wants, or does not want, in the matter of clothes. I should like to encourage the American in her shopping expeditions. I have seen her so sadly misunderstood, so sadly maligned in England. I have been by her side while she examined everything critically within eye and finger shot. I have seen, too, attentive people dismantle a window for her. I have heard her suave reply: 'Well, I guess I can find what I want elsewhere.' I believe that on one occasion I saved her life. I should advise her not to be discouraged, to go on. We are becoming used to her. And Harrod's, I believe, is surely built on just that large and generous plan which permits of wares being exhibited without fear of being purchased.

I do not mean to infer that Harrod's is all American. I merely affirm that there is as much American atmosphere in it as is good for anyone. And I have often been sorry for Americans while we held to our truly British notions of shop-keeping. We do not 'comfort' ourselves here as they do in America, but we are gradually working up to that standard of enjoyment. Harrod's delightful resting and reading room, telephones, charming lunch-room, sweetmeats, messenger-boys, theatre office, etc., all mean home to the American and comfort to us.

'Good clothes is everything when you 'ain't got 'em,' said a certain old lady. And the American without her green corn and ice-cream soda was a homesick woman in London.

Chapter VIII

Tailors and Dressmakers

WE have now come to the real difficulty which besets the shopper in London. So long as things are unmade, one has a wonderful and comfortable world of shops in which to buy. So long as one buys by the yard, life is an easy matter. Then comes the question of making up.

This is where one's best friend, after standing by one through a long pilgrimage, gracefully and pathetically deserts one. Say you have seen her in a nicely-cut gown—do you ever think she will let you know who made it? She will tell you how much she paid for the cloth, where she bought it, and give you any particulars with regard to that part of the business; but directly you begin to be eager regarding her dressmaker, you will see a wan look of distrust creep into her eyes, and she will steer off like a yacht taking a bad tack, and will discourse vaguely on the Wagner operas and the servant question. Likewise, if you come to London prepared to be recommended to a tailor or a good dressmaker who will take your wardrobe in hand, you will probably have no help whatever except from advertisements.

The most difficult person to find in London is just that obliging, moderate dressmaker who can cut and make clothes without either spoiling them or ruining you.

In all the well-known big shops you may get clothes well made. The difficulty is to get a number of clothes well made, and not to lose a fortune in the process. Every year the approximate cost of a dress goes up, every year it becomes more impossible to be without the dainty details which dressmakers delight to supply. Not so very long ago one might acquire even a tailor-made costume to order for 'six guineas.' Nowadays, however, when you try to get people to meet an estimate of this sort, everything which seems to make a dress attractive is left out. A costume without a silk lining is like a cake without fruit; yet, in every case of meeting an estimate, out goes the silk lining from the list of extras. Other things follow suit, until you are left with the skin of a dress and no adequate anatomy to it. Seven guineas (Oh, stranger to London!) will give you a silk-lined costume to order, nine guineas will trim it, fifteen will elaborate it with handwork, and twenty will make it a dream. Five guineas is really the difficult sum, and yet not so long ago it seemed sufficient.

For good tailoring one has to pay, and the attractive devise of '*From* five guineas,' in the end generally means very far from indeed.

London is intersected with tailoring establishments such as Dale's, who have places in Regent and Sloane Streets, Buckingham Palace and Gloucester Roads. This company really provides good workmanship at reasonable prices.

Marcus's, in Bond Street and Regent Street, are also to be much commended.

Queen's Road, Bayswater, is a first-rate place in which to find good tailors.

Dressmaking in any of the big shops may always be gauged by an estimate in the first instance. Good, private, cheap dressmakers are really family secrets, and cannot be mentioned here any more than in the sanctity of private conversation. They exist in remote and difficult spots, such as Shepherd's Bush and Camden Town. Whenever they move into illustrious parts they are immediately bitten with the desire to add and detract—prices in the first instance, trimmings in the second. The plea is always the same one—high rents, and the difficulty of living in fashionable London. After that it is once more cake without fruit, or high bills for all of us. The real, main, and completed difficulty in London is the dressmaking difficulty.

Until your London is well known to you, it is much the best thing to go to the shops themselves and place yourself in their hands. The one secret to be disclosed is that even in suburban large drapers' shops they have excellent staffs of dressmakers, and no one need despise the shops that are not entirely of the West before one has first sampled their dressmaking establishment.

Chapter IX

Chapter de Luxe

It is, of course, to be presumed that everyone who reads this book is not barred by circumstances from entering the portals of certain places up to now mentioned with the reserve born of a longing which only money can satisfy.

In speaking of Sloane Street, for instance, I passed over such luxurious places as Blanche's for exquisite hats, Hubert Beach for tailoring, 'Elfrida' and 'Mirette' for the daintiest wares in toques, and Jerrion's for tailoring and dressmaking, and Christie's for real lace in delightful examples.

These shops only display exquisite things, and it is not to be expected that they fit into a workaday world. In their own sphere they are perfect, and London in certain parts is dotted with their kind. Fenwick, in Bond Street; Haywards, Russell and Allenby; and in the intersecting streets there Redfern, Durrant and Thomas, are people who may only be mentioned in a Chapter de Luxe. Jay's I have already spoken of in this connection, and Ernest and Fisher in Regent Street, John Simmons in the Haymarket.

Furs bought at Victory's, or the International in Regent Street, at the Grafton in Bond Street, are exquisite and luxurious things.

Chapter X

Colour

HAVE you ever tried to discern the real, vital difference between one shop and another? And have you ever discovered that a very vital difference lies in *colour?* A beautiful sense of colour makes a buyer—I mean a wholesale buyer—buy a beautiful quality of stuff. I think he cannot possibly help himself. The fact remains that the two, good colour and fine quality, almost invariably go together.

I do not suppose, for instance, that the principal buyer in Woolland's could possibly resist a nice piece of colour any more than an artistically-minded woman could resist relieving him of it. They set their standard—such an article and such a place—and you thereupon get a whole business to correspond with it. The people going in and out of Woolland's—passing the windows even—are, in a sense, being trained to that nice idea of colour. Sloane Street is in line with a like regard for harmony. The dissonant notes are elsewhere. It is impossible, for instance, to buy anything in Brixton which is not guaranteed to show up well in a 700 candle-power arc-lamp.

Some parts of London are lighted in this way. *You have to buy your goods accordingly.* There is nothing like a good dairy-maid pink for 7,000 candle arc-lamp power, therefore the particularly well-lighted suburbs gradually clothe themselves in radiant pink. On the other hand, a gentle subdued yellow light throws a glamour of Liberty over colour. The result at Liberty's is a 'key' of colour, a trifle more warm than ordinary daylight justifies. I always watch my light when I am buying dress material. A picture to be exhibited is not of more consequence than the tone of a dress.

On a counter of relative and contrasting colours a colour may seem distinguished which, with its proper background, has no distinction at all. Dairy-maid pink becomes a violent, ill-natured thing when not in competition with arc-lamps and sky-blues. It would really be wise to give this spinster's suburban joy a long and hallowed rest. My complaint is that we are so dependent on the taste of the gentlemen who buy these things and light their shops accordingly. For a long time these people never moved beyond what I should call the maroon and navy-blue stage. No shopkeeper in London had an idea past these two colours. Think what slaves we were to the gentlemen who bought for us in the early seventies! They liked to see their own womenkind in black satin brocade and bombazine. And they had not a thought for anybody else.

Then came Liberty, and can anybody ever be grateful enough for that relief? With the refinement in colouring appeared refinement of texture, which in the receding year has been unparalleled in manufactures. Nothing Eastern or Oriental can show more delicious things than our own modern crêpons, chiffons, and silks. The refinement is due as much to discoveries in colour as to discoveries in manufacture. Delicate colours demand delicate material. The thing is done much more easily than one could ever imagine.

There are still shops in London, however, which treasure the maroon traditions. There is no need to warn you—you will recognise them at a glance. But once discover your 'colour' shop, selection is an easier matter. The knowledge and satisfaction of it makes me wish that every buyer in London should have his colour scheme tested periodically by a kind of inspectorship, as necessary to our artistic development as a County Council is to our knowledge of sanitation and reform. As a preliminary, I should always march them at least once a year through Woolland's in Knightsbridge.

Chapter XI

A Chapter on Shoes

With Sidelights on the Fiscal Policy

WHILE it may be said that in London you may turn into any shop and buy gloves, it is impossible that you may turn into any shop and buy shoes. Ill-fitting gloves, at a pinch, may serve, but ill-fitting shoes, especially at a pinch, are a tragedy.

This being a book whose main endeavour, though narrowed by circumstances, is to be critical, the chance now exhibits itself for saying something definite about English shoes. It is safe to be critical, because things in this connection are now more on a tip-top footing than they were, say eight years ago, when a chapter like this might have been held libellous. Until the American invasion the state of the ready-made shoe market in England, as far as the Englishwoman was concerned, was painful in the extreme. Shoes were made to fit 'lasts,' not feet, and the exact sizes of these lasts were 'stock sizes,' handed down from the reign of the Georges.

Feet at this period, we are persuaded, from the study of records and prints, and also in the early Victorian period, if we may trust our daguerreotypes, were unnoted for æsthetic outline.

Presumably, they served for the lasts of the times.

It seems incredible that our great-grandmothers, until quite recently, could gauge the market of modern shoes just as easily as they did in their youth. The same twos, threes, fives, sixes, etc., did duty for her as for us, until the advent of the American! Who can ever forget it?

I have seen one firm grow all over the land, like daisies blooming in a green meadow, a shop appearing in every district. It originated in London, it moved to the provinces. In a spare hour or two at a Scotch town one found these people. The same shop, windows, the same neat shelves, the same adaptable ladders, the same up-to-date trying-on appliances. What is more—and this I look on as a real discovery—there was the same pioneering shopman. There are people who remember that person with something like real passionate admiration. He was sent round, I should fancy, by the American nation, as a pioneer missionary to save the benighted English-woman.

Did he not teach some of us for the first time in our lives that shoes ought to fit feet, not feet fit shoes?

Compare our methods: 'Madame, this shoe fits you perfectly.' Then think of our pioneer. I saw this particular person taking the word of a whole shopful of women as to whether his shoes fitted them or not. He never once dictated, never once questioned their statements. I saw him move concernedly from one to another, ordering flying serving people to bring down more and yet more from the boot-shelves. Half sizes, quarter sizes, fractional sizes; shoes that fitted glove-like over the top of the foot, shoes with boxed toes, shoes with welts and shoes without welts—there was nothing that this pleasant, quick, alert individual did not place at one's disposal.

It is not surprising that everyone bought shoes. It is not surprising that after buying they liked their purchases.

American shoes have revolutionized us. It is not because better leather is used. British material in any trade is generally excellent. But British conservatism in the outline of the model of shoes, and antiquated machinery in the making of them, allowed several American firms to coin a fortune in England. As Englishwomen, we now benefit exceedingly from this conflict in the emotion of manufactures. English shoemakers endeavour to acquire the well-shaped lightness of American shoes, while Americans adapt the willowy, skeleton appearance of the American to the drawing of the English foot. There is discrimination required. A shoe labelled 'American' is not necessarily a Hannan, or something equally distinguished. It may be Northampton, with needle-point toe. The newest Americans are not needle-pointed.

The Anglo-American Shoe Company in Regent Street mixes the average very nicely. Here you have most of the results of the competition, and there is really something from which to choose. Boots and shoes of all descriptions are to be had in this, I think the first shop to import Americans. It is useful to note that slippers as we wear them in England are not worn in America. Nearly all house-shoes worn there cover the instep as do our outdoor ones. French and Austrian slippers are still the finest, from an artistic point of view.

The London Shoe Company in Bond Street and Sloane Street gives the very best selection in slippers. These run from their specially cheap and nice black satin house-slippers to the most elaborate beaded and embroidered ones. And if you want real 'finds' at any odd time, Peter Jones in Sloane Square has a marvellous way of importing 'rarities.' Austrian slippers in unusual colours and design, bargains in shoes, are to be had here.

Lillie and Skinner is an established boot and shoe place, with a definite reputation for having a big selection from which to choose. Randall's shops are well over London and known popularly.

A very charming bedroom slipper with unbacked heels, in pretty colours of pink and blue, and any shade in satin, are to be had at an all-round price of 7s. 6d. in The Incroyable Shoe Shop in Oxford Street. These are really dainty things.

And as for the Americans, go to the first 'Walk-over,' 'Sirosis,' 'Signet' shop you can find. If an American attends to you, you may spend each afternoon trying on his wares, and you are likely to uphold his brand of shoe for ever.

'Sirosis' came in with needle-points, but they have changed that with the march of fashion. 'Walk-overs' strode in with a breadth of toe which exaggerated the suddenness of the change. Now, however, everything is moderately rounded in both cases. Real American shoes are made to be worn with rubbers in wet weather. Englishwomen must remember this if their Americans 'let in.' The shoes sold in this country are now as a rule made to agree more readily with the climate.

Hannans are one of the finest, and are to be had in shops which make a point of selling the best American sorts.

A Chapter on Shoes

Away from the ready-made, there is no country like England for boots and shoes made to order, and no city like London for getting these at their best. A shoe made at Yapp's in Sloane Street, Myckoff in Regent Street, Dobbie's in Piccadilly, is really a work of art, and not to be surpassed in the length or breadth of America. This I can personally testify to, for in America I once had such a pair of shoes at an American for repairs, and his delight over the beauty of the leather, the carefulness of the workmanship, and the general appearance of the whole, was quite frank and cosmopolitan, and altogether genuine.

Chapter XII

Explorations

THIS is the chapter in which we pick out at random the opportunities which one may miss by not knowing one's London, by passing, perhaps daily, in an omnibus shops known to the pedestrian, by living too near one part and not enough in the next—in short, the opportunities which exist for the Londoner, and are out of question for the ordinary visitor.

Who would ever have thought of finding garnets in the Strand, for instance, artistically set in pretty modern settings?—an old friend with a very new face, and nobody to show it to you.

The shop which sells garnets, and has nothing else in its window, is quite near the Cecil, so perhaps my news is not news to every visitor.

Then, to hark back to Knightsbridge, if you are tired of tea every day in Kensington Gardens, turn into an arcade let into the new triangular buildings at Knightsbridge, and find under a singularly inartistic glass dome a singularly artistic little group of lady shop-keepers, one of whom has a delightful tea-shop. I proclaim it over the length and breadth of London that here one may get genuine Scotch scones, properly baked and properly hot. Next door is a dressmaker's establishment, with a good reputation for pretty and skilful work.

And showing all over these shops is the evident genius of one designer, Miss Pamela Coleman Smith, who owns a little shop in the same arcade. This place ought to be visited by everyone who likes to see character artistically displaying itself. It is full of quaint hand-coloured prints, books and pictures. Go there for Christmas cards, menus, and everything of this sort which you do not want to see repeated at every point in London.

And while I am on the exploring tack, let me recommend a frame-maker's of real renown. Rowley, in Silver Street, Kensington, as a framer of prints, photographs, etc., has an expert way of doing things more quickly and moderately than any frame-maker I have known.

Tottenham Court Road is the highway for furniture, but bargains in old furniture in London are not now to be had. The rage for ancient things has not only put a fanciful price on genuine old stuff, it has fictitiously influenced anything that is second-hand.

The quaint shops of Chelsea are delightful, but all very wide-awake in this connection. Church Street, in Kensington, for old silver, china, and furniture, is a little picture-show by itself.

The artist's hand in this trade, however, is, while not losing its cunning, losing some of its opportunity, for every large and influential furniture establishment has now its special show-rooms for the antique.

A most useful shop for beads to be bought for any kind of odd purpose is A. Cameron's and Co., at 9, Cranbourne Street, almost next to the Hippodrome.

At 34, Soho, is a good little Italian place where one may buy all kinds of provisions not included in the usual stores catalogue.

Pickard's, in Regent Street, is an invaluable place for wedding-presents. Although this place is mainly one devoted to the selling of things manufactured for the making of good coffee, there are delightful things besides to be bought here which are not to be discovered elsewhere. Little casseroles in silver frames, Vienna coffee-pots in ware or silver, coffee-cups on tray, etc.—all these are to be had here. I understand, to account for the novelty of many of these, that there are Pickard's patents attached to most of them. This shop is a unique one in many respects.

The best place for china and glass is Oxford and New Oxford Street. Here we may get things matched more easily than elsewhere. Shops devoted to this business alone are dotted along the streets.

One could run on with many places, but I refrain from more than a mere suggestion of some of them.

Chapter XIII

Sales

THE magic word that stocks our wardrobes, deletes our purses, disorganizes our routine, fascinates us, repels us, delights us, disappoints us twice a year regularly in London—for how much is it not answerable?

The ethics of sales are so disturbing, one time so morally and clearly good, the next minute so conspicuously disappointing and bad, that no woman, I believe, is quite settled in her mind regarding them.

Personally, I find it a delightful thing to buy a pretty piece of stuff 'marked down.' Even when I can buy the same thing fresh and by the yard, and at the identical price, it never thrills me as does that remnant with the wrong amount of yards, the torn edge, and the *marked down price*. There is no doubt we all love a bargain, even when it is only on paper.

This trait in our feminine character is fully appreciated by the shopkeeper. Therefore, there are sometimes disappointments to be encountered at sales. On the other hand, some of us attempt to remain level-headed in the matter, and are not to be won over.

Correspondingly, sales are our happy hunting-grounds. Taken in a sensible way, sales are a necessity to the modern woman, just as certainly as they are a necessity to the modern shopkeeper. They are to her the stock-making time, just as they are the shopkeepers stocktaking. She gracefully relieves him of the things which would not last

another season's shop-wear, but are quite ready for being exhibited elsewhere. The best policy for a woman is to frequent the places at sale-time which are barred by expensiveness in the full season. Good houses really reduce their prices, and sell the goods which they have already selected with care and supreme judgment at wonderfully lowered prices. It is to their advantage to sell these at the end of a season. But only the finest houses can afford to let prices go down very far for a mere fashion. One has to remember this at sale-times. The shops which have no tremendous stock of things certainly must find themselves out of 'sale and surplus' stock just at the most exciting times and at this point no doubt buy wildly those 'especially cheap lines' prepared by manufacturers for such an emergency.

Then one may buy reticules by the half-dozen at a shilling each which had better never been seen in London; rustling silks of brave appearance and tinselly quality are rushed at with avidity. The fever of the bargain gets on the crowd, and the fight begins. At the end of the day the weary fighters look over their wares at home.

Alas! the reticules are already showing signs of leakage, the rustling silks demonstrate where the first cuts will appear. Life becomes a horrid mockery to the time of so many good shillings wasted. The day is closed with feminine and forcible maledictions on the ethics and practices of sales.

Now, no guide is more needed by the visitor to London than a guide to the sales. There is a tide on the first Monday or so in January which you can almost follow in the buses. It proceeds to 'Marshall's,' to 'Peter Robinson's,' and my own tide always flows steadily as well to Knightsbridge. Pick out all the newest, most fashionable places in London, and frequent these devotedly. You not only find bargains, you find things displayed *en masse* which cannot be seen in such variety and profusion at any other part of a tidy year. Then is the time for finding models, chic coats, and pretty underwear.

The real advice to be given with regard to sales is to shop at this period in the very finest houses in London. You will never regret a bargain found, say, at Jay's, at Redmayne's, Lewis and Allenby's, Simmons', of the Haymarket, or Russell and Allen's.

Chapter XIV

Luncheon and Tea Rooms

It is a long time since Mrs. Carlyle discovered that a chop and a glass of stout at "Verrey's" afforded a pleasant change to the routine of house life. "It amuses me, besides keeping me in health," she declared.

Poor days when they had no tea-rooms! Yet the thin end of the wedge was a stray luncheon place or two where ladies might eat a meal outside of their own homes and independently of the invitation of others. Nowadays our shopping area is so extended, our time so limited, our comfort and health of so much more reasonable consideration than formally, that London is dotted with delightful luncheon and tea rooms which are daily crowded to the doors. Historically, the A.B.C. shops present the finest reputation. They solved the woman's problem, giving her tea when she wanted it and where she wanted it—where in this case meaning everywhere.

London caught on, as it were, with spirit, and

buckets of tea became the rage. Then came moderation, in the case of delightful little rooms like the tea-room in Dickens and Jones' ! Finally came elaboration, in such cases as the pink-studded tea-rooms of Bond Street. Only now are we striking the happy medium—like the Dickens and Jones medium—to great advantage. Large cups of tea, plenty of milk, marble-topped tables, and Alpine structures of cake, are going out. Little brown teapots, hot water, small cups, little cakes, nice bread and butter, are coming in.

They have come in more reasonably and daintily in High Street, Kensington, than in any place in London. Try what is called a "cold scone (it is really hot with fresh baking) and butter" at Derry and Toms' old English tea-rooms, and see if there is anything quite so nice in London. Or turn into Hill's on your way to Kensington Gardens, and take tea as quietly and comfortably as in your own drawing-room, or to Fullers' windows overlooking the drive up Kensington Palace Gardens, and eat walnut cream cake. All of these places are delightful.

Lunch also at Derry and Toms' and Hill's—they

understand there the delightfulness of light lunches as well as mcre weighty affairs. The finest ladies' luncheon-place in London I should say is Harrod's. That it appeals to stronger appetites is evident from the men who also frequent it. Everything here is delightfully served. I have memories of single cutlets from a silver grill! Where else in London may a lady have a single cutlet if she wants it? We are a healthier crowd than the "poached-egg-and-bun" girl of recent days, yet we still like small things, and very seldom even yet can we get them. In Harrods' they have everything, even small things.

Woolland's, near at hand, has also a luncheon-place, small but very dainty, and tea here in the afternoon is delightful.

In town, one of the latest additions to tea-rooms is that busy place—on matinées especially—the Kardomah in Piccadilly, near the bottom of Bond Street. In this place they strike the happy medium between Bond Street and *buckets* both as regards price and management. Coffee here is excellent.

Stewart's, close at hand, with another shop in Bond Street, is quite in accordance with Bond Street traditions, but not arrogantly so. Everything here is delicious.

The Cottage Tea-Rooms, near Piccadilly Circus, are run by New Zealand ladies, and well known to colonials and their friends. This place is on the shilling tea average, and very nice at that. The Far

East in Regent Street averages from sixpence for tea alone and eatables accordingly. It is nicely attended to and very popular. Fuller's will always remain a favourite with those who like tea daintily served. Those who resent the shilling average will approve of Fuller's. This is not on the scale of either the very expensive or the very cheap. The rooms are not only comfortable, but dainty—how well they know the needs of a woman there!

Liberty's have a little room for tea and biscuits (quite cheap). It is really the Far East, with more of the genuine atmosphere than is generally dispersed in such places.

Peter Robinson's and Evans' have nice luncheon and tea rooms. Force of habit makes me commend Dickens and Jones'. I can never forget their shining coffee kettles nor the quality of their tea. You may buy it by the pound after you have tried it. I generally do, after a cup there.

Adjacent to the Queen's Hall, in Upper Regent Street, are the Rose Tea-Rooms—very convenient after concerts, very dainty, and again on the shilling average. In Bond Street, the Old Oak Tea-Rooms are charming, the Ladies' Own Tea Association very popular. Tea-rooms here spring up like muffled mushrooms in a night. Everything is complete to the quality of the music, which is restrained and refined almost to fainting-point. There is sometimes a lady palmist on the premises.

Then whiff, in a night, little Aladdin's miniature palace disappears, and in its stead, behold a blouse shop, or somebody selling prints and rarities. The history of these places is sudden and sharp and severe, but we still go on having experimental tea-shops in Bond Street.

These already well established are delightful, though often in miniature. We all need a little more air and a little less tea in Bond Street.

Chapter XV

Hotels for Shoppers

IF you ever ask a question about hotels in London, you will invariably be answered, 'London is *rich* in hotels.' So it is—wealthy. But for the lady in town for a night or two palaces may be deserts, and elaboration only a discomfort. There is always the demand for comfort and quietness, for hotels neither given over only to the glittering task of impressing one with overwhelming splendour nor to that desolate one of entertaining the commercial traveller. For a long time there seemed to be only the two extremes in London hotels. Now we are embarked on a new era.

Comfortable, bright, and splendid little hotels—little beside the enormity of a fascinating Cecil, a glittering white and beautiful Savoy, a towering Metropole, capacious Grand, a spacious Victoria, and an elaborate Hyde Park—have sprung up in and out amongst the newer things of London. They are delightful for the lady shopper.

The Kenilworth, in Great Russell Street, is a favourite with at least a dozen of my acquaintances. Everything is moderately right for a lady, inexpensive and delightful. A number of hotels of the same order ought really to be taken alphabetically, because their claims to popularity are nearly identical.

In connection with the Kenilworth is the Waverley Hotel in Southampton Row. This old London thoroughfare is dotted with good places. There is the temperance West Central, which has been much added to and improved.

Close by is the Bedford, a delightful little hotel, with pretty coffee-rooms and a particularly nice grill-room.

A comparatively new set of temperance hotels — the Esmond in Montagu Street, Thackeray in Russell Square, and Kingsley in Hart Street — are all excellent. There one may live at inclusive charges of from 8s. 6d. to 10s. 6d. per day, with all the comforts attached, as a rule, to more expensive establishments.

A very delightful and quiet hotel is the Howard in Norfolk Street, Strand. The streets here down to the Embankment are dotted with pleasant and quiet places of a like calibre. Formerly it used to be a difficult thing for a lady to discover a quiet hotel where, as I have said before, she might find a more varied cuisine than that appointed in remote ages, established and adhered to for the benefit of the commercial traveller and nobody else on earth. Our days of oil-cloth, large steaks and stout are over, even in reasonable establishments; and the latest and nicest evidences of the wish to cater as well for ladies are very fully to be appreciated in such hotels as I have mentioned.

Chapter XVI

Entr'actes

A LITTLE pleasure along with all this detail of business is what a woman generally manages to obtain. A morning's shopping, lunch, and a matinée—there is her programme. It is useful, therefore, to include in these chapters a few hints on the dispositions of theatres. One would not like to know, for instance, that seats may be booked at the Haymarket for half a crown, and at His Majesty's for so low a fee as two shillings. There is hardly a theatre in America which does not provide a good seat for like sums, booked in advance. But in England, for the most part, one has to depend on the pit for anything below four shillings. It is still the custom of English women to take their pleasures in moderation, and the evidence of this is the long queue of waiting people at the pit-doors on matinée days.

His Majesty's possesses such a roomy pit, with so much accommodation, that you need not be unduly alarmed if you take your places pretty well down the line. The Criterion, on the other hand, is a much older theatre, and space is restricted. Also, the stairway down to an inner door is left open for the accommodation of the crowd, so that if you are well out in the pavement there is small chance of your finding a seat. Wyndham's and the New Theatres have both nice waiting-places, and so long as one is compelled to follow this practise for finding a half-crown seat, so long will the little afford pleasant surroundings during that long half-hour. Half-an-hour wait is usually long enough outside for a moderately successful play, but where there is a run on things like Mr. Waller's presentation of 'Henry V.' at the Imperial, over an hour is often necessary.

The Garrick Theatre has a wide pit, with plenty of room, the Duke of York's also. The Vaudeville in the Strand has a particularly small pit in a bijou house, so that we must always be in very good time at this place.

It is not always known that there are matinées at Christmas-time in the Palace, Hippodrome, etc.; that seats there are much more easily procured, and much more comfortable, than in the usual cheap seats of theatres. It is possible for ladies to attend the performances there with great comfort and pleasure.

Chapter XVII

If I had —— Pounds to Spend

THE morals, it is declared, are a matter of geography, wealth of comparison; and shopping, after all, and despite the details contained in this book, is purely a matter of how much money you carry in your pocket. Therefore, to be advised to shop in Sloane Street when you possess merely a five-pound note is information more picturesque than necessary. To be told where to shop when you have that amount of money is more to the point. In consequence, I devote one more chapter to giving you your locality according to your means, and to find the average. I shall first suppose that you are buying a season's full wardrobe for, say, first £20, and after that for £50.

I should never be afraid of the £20 basis to do my shopping partly in Regent Street.

I should like to arrange something of this sort:

A short skirt and coat in Peter Robinson's.
A smart kit-cat hat to match.
A black evening dress there also.
One dressy blouse in La Samaritaine.
One linen skirt and coat in Wallace Taylor's.
Two delaine or linen blouses in Westbourne Grove.
Lingerie here also.
Shoes in the 'Walk-over.'
Stockings in Penberthy's.
Dozen underwear here also.
Slippers at Peter Jones'.
Gloves at Harrod's or Russell's, in Wardour Street.

Then after that I should begin to put things together. If I had managed economically I should now buy dress-stuffs at Woolland's, trimmings at Owen's, lace at Swan and Edgar's, and silk lining at Whiteley's.

Handkerchiefs I should buy at Walpole's, under-skirts at Evans'. And while I was in the last place I should buy an untrimmed hat, and trim it from Oxford Street. Veils, etc., I should also acquire here.

These are prejudiced views, I know, but this is a prejudiced book.

On the £50 basis. I should still make sure of my

morning neat costume at Peter Robinson's, and also my evening skirt. I should still court Penberthy's for underwear, and I should still buy dress-stuffs at Woolland's. But for hats I should venture into Wigmore or Sloane Streets, and try some of the places I have mentioned as having their stated prices. I should endeavour to have one pair of good English shoes made for me, and also court attention from the Americans. I should buy lace at Baker's, and have a gown made at Derry and Toms'.

I should find my best lingerie in Sloane Street, and all out-of-door wraps at Harvey Nichol's. In this more exalted position I should not mind observing a sale of French dressing-gowns at Whiteley's, and making up my wardrobe with a pretty thing from there. I should also be particularly observant of blouse sales at Barker's; otherwise, I should certainly include two blouses from Sloane Street, one being tailor-made and chic, and another loose and dressy.

I should like a still higher margin from Bond Street, and higher still for the famous dressmaker whose one bill would swamp these two much-dissected sums. But there are plenty of people who love to search the shops to meet these sums, and it is for the benefit of them in particular that this small book has been written.

Chapter XVIII

Hints to Shopkeepers

WAAL! Anything else you've got on your mind?'

That question, once fired at an Englishwoman in an American store, paralyzed her shopping activities for an entire afternoon. It surely demonstrates to shopkeepers how carefully we, their indispensable patrons, ought to be treated.

There is a league amongst us, a secret society. Our tactics and our politics never appear even in the ladies' papers, but our influence is everywhere. We are in the habit of recommending or condemning you to our friends, all because of your treatment of us. Your businesses rise and fall accordingly as we are pleased or not pleased, and not always so much on account of the goods you sell as on account of the way you do it.

When, for instance, I went to a new place and tried to match, if you remember, a certain shade of ribbon! Your ribbon was not my colour, I informed your young lady in smart attire. Nothing changed in her except her deportment towards me, and that was like the sudden opening of a draughty door. Indignantly she rapped twice on the counter with an extremely injured and stumpy pencil—which had evidently done some work of this sort before—producing YOU.

'The lady says the colours do not match,' declared your affronted young person.

YOU — an inquisition in frock-coat — examining them, had the audacity to declare:

'Madame, this is just the thing you want.'

I left you, rather icily on my part, if you remember, and I never went to YOU again. What is more, I prevented several others from ever reaching you.

May I plead with you to remember that it is fatal to your success in life to tell a lady, 'Madame, this is just the thing you want,' when she has signified her disappointment already; or, 'Madame, it matches perfectly,' when quite nicely she has given her opinion that it does not match at all.

There must be no altercation on these points. We must neither be dictated to nor over-persuaded. That person who comes in answer to the sharp double rap is a minor impertinence to all of us. The occasional visitor must not take him seriously. 'The lady says she merely wanted to look at it,' cries the lady with the pencil. Well, how can one like or dislike a thing until one has seen it? 'Sir, your business is fourth-rate, and doomed!' I could inform YOU wherever you proceed on such tactics. You may bully us into buying once or twice, but do you ever realize how much we dislike you for having persuaded us against our inclinations, or how little we dream of ever going near you again?

Your best policy, in the first instance, is not so much to sell as to please. Even an American will begin to buy in bulk wherever she is sufficiently enchanted. We do not need much inducement beyond the ravishing things you spread out for us. These are quite enough of a temptation as they stand. Therefore, to such of you who are left who still approve of these quaint, police-like methods, let us inform you, we informally and everywhere condemn you.

Also, we are not so easily deceived in small matters as you might think. When we see a costume marked 'Exclusive,' we are inclined to remember that just the day before it had been labelled, 'To be had in all colours.' How sweetly I have seen '*Le dernier cri*' reposing on a worn-out season's first pride! The power to alter fashions of a window-dresser may be enormous, but somehow it does not always convince us.

I should like also to point out that the black crêpe-de-chine effect of the assistants in some fashionable shops is not the most encouraging agency through which to be induced to buy clothes. These faultlessly-gowned people, though probably much more smartly dressed than the majority of their customers, do not impress us with an overwhelming desire to buy something just as fine. Do you not know that sometimes this very elegance prevents our buying anything at all?

Traveller to London, do not be afraid of these people! When the crêpe-de-chine is laid aside, I expect they have their human feelings like the rest of us. And, in reality, they are often most kind and helpful. But if I were in the responsible position of a leading London shopkeeper, I should do away with this starchy sort of artificial-looking service, and have all my assistants in a trig and pretty uniform, which would, I think, be much more delightful to them, and certainly less disconcerting to us.

BILLING AND SONS, LTD., PRINTERS, GUILDFORD

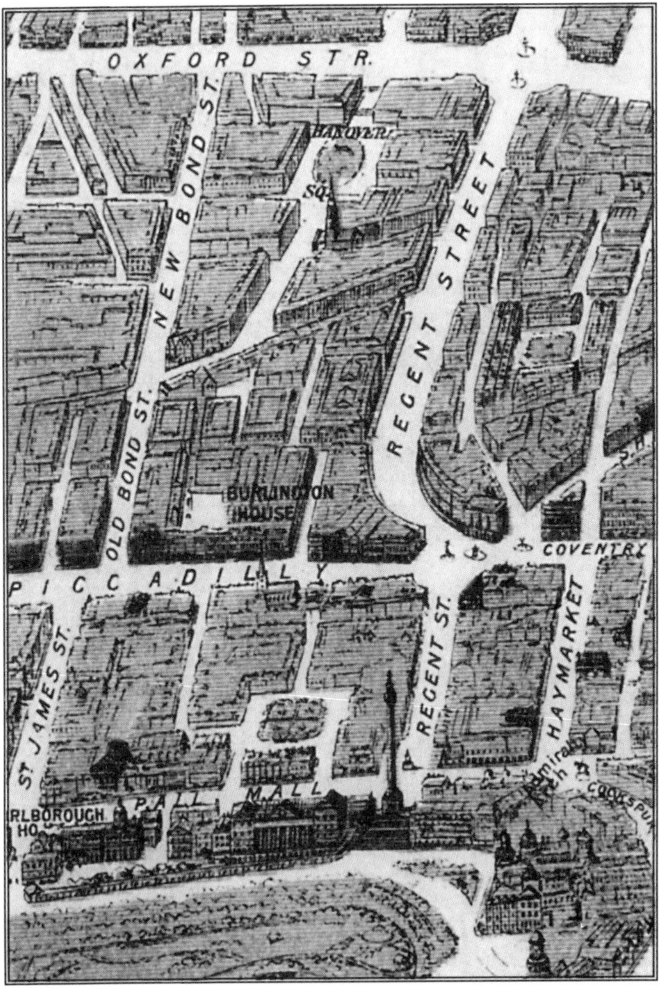
OXFORD STR.
NEW BOND ST.
HANOVER
SQ.
REGENT STREET
OLD BOND ST.
BURLINGTON HOUSE
COVENTRY
PICCADILLY
ST. JAMES ST.
REGENT ST.
HAYMARKET
REGENT ST.
PALL MALL
Admiralty Arch
RLBOROUGH HO.

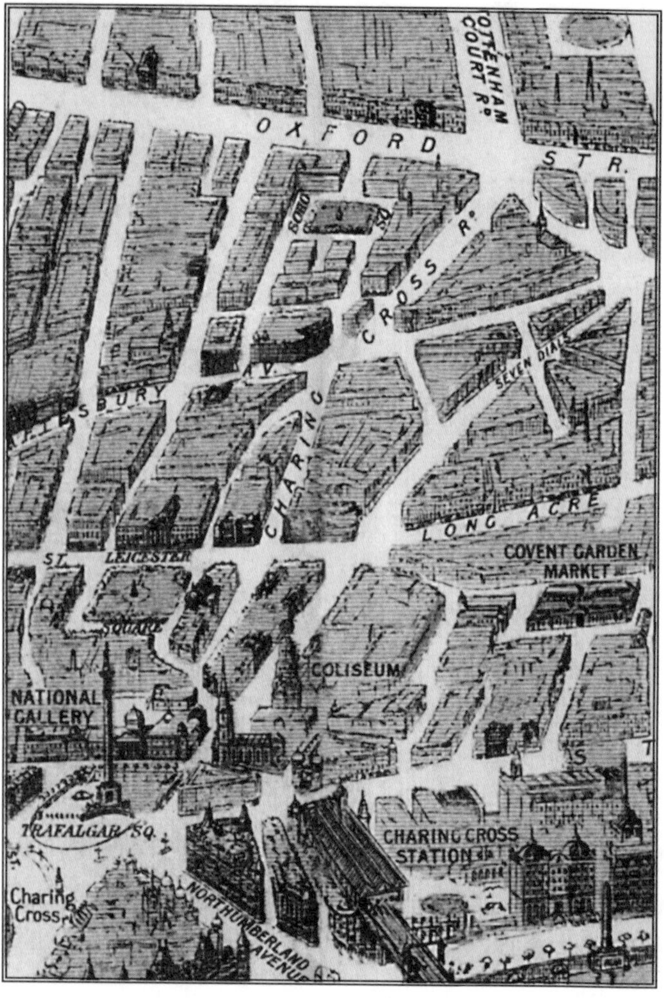
OXFORD STR.
TOTTENHAM COURT Rd
SOHO SQ.
CHARING CROSS Rd
SEVEN DIALS
LONG ACRE
COVENT GARDEN MARKET
LEICESTER SQUARE
ST.
COLISEUM
NATIONAL GALLERY
TRAFALGAR SQ.
Charing Cross
NORTHUMBERLAND AVENUE
CHARING CROSS STATION

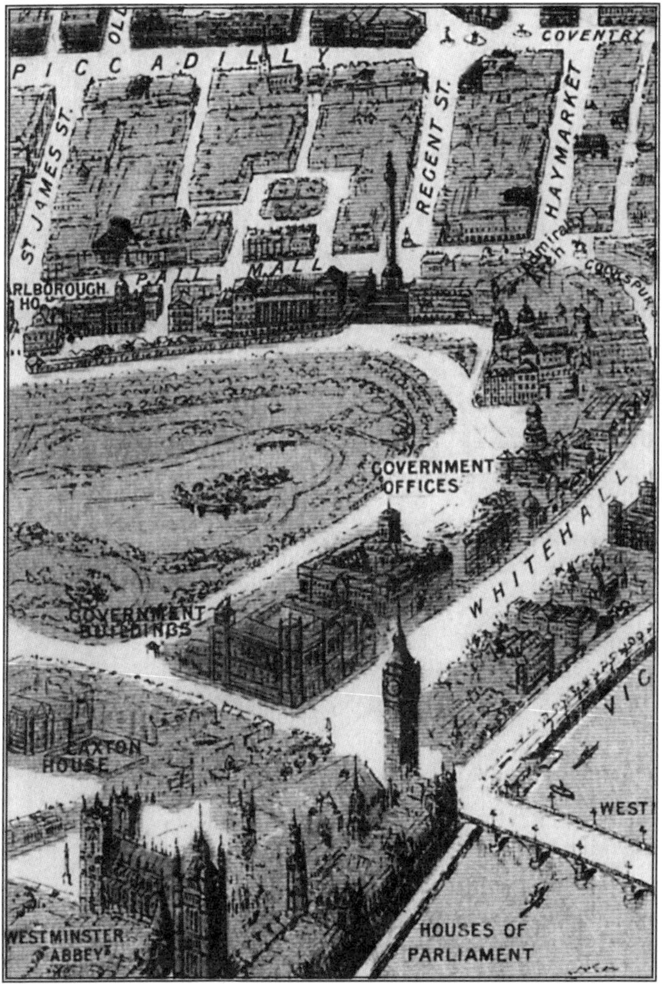
COVENTRY
PICCADILLY
OLD
ST JAMES ST.
REGENT ST.
HAYMARKET
PALL MALL
ARLBOROUGH HO
Admiralty Arch
COCKSPUR
GOVERNMENT OFFICES
WHITEHALL
GOVERNMENT BUILDINGS
CAXTON HOUSE
VIC
WEST
WESTMINSTER ABBEY
HOUSES OF PARLIAMENT

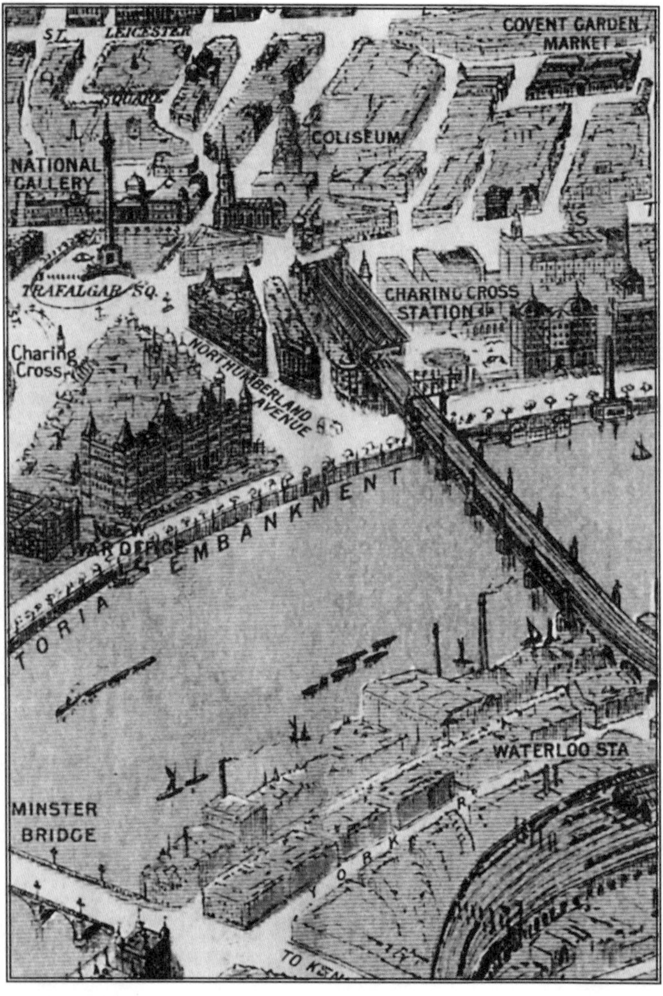

COVENT GARDEN MARKET
ST. LEICESTER SQUARE
COLISEUM
NATIONAL GALLERY
TRAFALGAR SQ.
CHARING CROSS STATION
Charing Cross
NORTHUMBERLAND AVENUE
NEW WAR OFFICE
TORIA EMBANKMENT
WATERLOO STA
MINSTER BRIDGE
YORK R
TO KEN